3 MINUTES A DAY FROM EASTER TO PENTECOST

A Daily Devotional with Reflections, Prayer, and Activities

BY
JOEL PRINTS

Copyright © 2024 by JOEL PRINTS

All rights reserved. No part of this publication may be reproduced, stored or
transmitted in any form or by any means, electronic, mechanical,
photocopying, recording, scanning, or otherwise without written permission
from the publisher. It is illegal to copy this book, post it to a website, or
distribute it by any other means without permission.

First edition

TABLE OF CONTENTS

INTRODUCTION
Day 1: Embracing Renewal
Day 2: Journeying Towards Hope
Day 3: Cultivating Gratitude
Day 4: Celebrating Resurrection
Day 5: Living in Light
Day 6: Extending Forgiveness
Day 7: Nurturing Seeds of Faith
Day 8: Watering Our Souls
Day 9: Bearing Fruit
Day 10: Receiving the Spirit
Day 11: Empowered for Mission
Day 12: Continuing the Journey
Day 13: Seeking Wisdom
Day 14: Trusting in God's Provision
Day 15: Walking in Obedience
Day 16: Loving Our Neighbors
Day 17: Showing Kindness
Day 18: Extending Mercy
Day 19: Building Unity
Day 20: Honoring Family
Day 21: Reconciliation and Restoration
Day 22: Sharing the Gospel
Day 23: Planting Seeds of Hope
Day 24: Cultivating Joy
Day 25: Counting Blessings

Day 26: Expressing Thankfulness
Day 27: Gratitude in Adversity
Day 28: Seeking Rest
Day 29: Trusting in God's Provision
Day 30: Finding Strength in Weakness
Day 31: Renewing Our Minds
Day 32: Reflecting on God's Love
Day 33: Revisiting Our Purpose
Day 34: Committing to Holiness
Day 35: Embracing Spiritual Disciplines
Day 36: Surrendering All to God
Day 37: Empowering Others
Day 38: Encouraging the Faint-hearted
Day 39: Sharing Our Testimony
Day 40: Cultivating a Heart of Gratitude
Day 41: Overflowing with Generosity
Day 42: Investing in Eternal Rewards
Day 43: Anticipating Christ's Return
Day 44: Preparing Our Hearts
Day 45: Watching and Praying
Day 46: Celebrating God's Faithfulness
Day 47: Commemorating God's Miracles
Day 48: Rejoicing in Eternal Victory
Day 49: Reflecting on the Journey
Day 50: Committing to Ongoing Growth
CONCLUSION

INTRODUCTION

For Christians, Easter and Pentecost are two of the most important times of the year. Easter celebrates the resurrection of Jesus Christ, while Pentecost commemorates the coming of the Holy Spirit. These seasons offer Christians an opportunity to reflect on the deeper meaning of their faith and to seek a closer relationship with God. This book is a daily devotional designed to help you make the most of these special seasons.
Each day, you'll find a brief reflection based on scripture passages related to Easter and Pentecost, along with a prayer to guide your thoughts and intentions. Additionally, each day includes an activity to engage your heart, mind, and spirit in a practical way, helping you to apply the insights gained from your reflection and prayer into your daily life.

Whether you're a seasoned believer or new to the Christian faith, this devotional is crafted to meet you where you are on your spiritual journey. It offers a space for contemplation, inspiration, and action, inviting you to deepen your understanding of God's love and grace.

As you embark on this 50-day journey from Easter to Pentecost, may you experience a renewed sense of hope, joy, and empowerment as you encounter the risen Christ and the transforming power of the Holy Spirit in your life. Let this devotional be a companion on your path of faith, guiding you closer to God's presence and purpose for you.

Day 1: Embracing Renewal

Reflection: Embracing the Season of Change

In this fast-paced world, change is inevitable. Yet, amidst the chaos of life's transitions, there lies an opportunity for renewal. Just as nature sheds its old leaves in preparation for new growth, we too can embrace the spirit of renewal during this season leading up to Easter. Reflect on Ecclesiastes 3:1-8, where it reminds us that there is a time for everything, including a time for change. Consider how you can embrace the changes in your life with grace and openness, trusting in God's plan for renewal.

Prayer: Inviting Renewal into Our Hearts

Almighty God, in this season of preparation, we come before you with hearts open to renewal. Help us to embrace the changes in our lives with courage and faith, knowing that you are with us every step of the way. Renew our spirits, O Lord, and guide us on the path of transformation. Amen.

Activity: Planting Seeds of Faith

As a symbolic gesture of renewal, take some time today to plant seeds of faith. Whether it's in a garden, a pot, or even a small indoor planter, sow seeds as a tangible reminder of the growth and renewal that is possible in our lives. As you nurture these seeds, reflect on how you can cultivate your faith and allow it to flourish in the days leading up to Easter.

Day 2: Journeying Towards Hope

Reflection: Finding Hope in the Unknown

Life's journey is often filled with twists and turns, and it's easy to feel lost or uncertain about the road ahead. Yet, in the midst of uncertainty, there is hope. Reflect on Romans 15:13, which reminds us that God is the source of hope, filling us with joy and peace as we trust in Him. Consider how you can find hope in the midst of life's uncertainties, knowing that God is with you every step of the way.

Prayer: Strengthening Our Faith Along the Journey

Heavenly Father, as we journey towards Easter, we are grateful for the hope that you provide. Strengthen our faith, O Lord, and fill us with your joy and peace. Guide us along the path of life, reassuring us of your presence and love. Help us to trust in you, even when the road ahead seems uncertain. Amen.

Activity: Creating a Hopeful Vision Board

Take some time today to create a vision board filled with images and words that inspire hope and faith. Include pictures of places you hope to visit, goals you hope to achieve, and quotes that uplift your spirit. Display this vision board in a prominent place where you can see it daily, reminding you of the hope that lies ahead on your journey towards Easter.

Day 3: Cultivating Gratitude

Reflection: Cultivating a Heart of Thanksgiving

In the midst of life's challenges, it's easy to focus on what we lack rather than what we have. Yet, cultivating a heart of gratitude can transform our perspective and fill us with joy. Reflect on 1 Thessalonians 5:16-18, where it encourages us to give thanks in all circumstances. Consider how you can cultivate a spirit of gratitude in your daily life, recognizing the blessings that surround you.

Prayer: Offering Gratitude for Blessings Past and Present

Gracious God, we come before you with hearts full of gratitude for the blessings you have bestowed upon us. Thank you for the gift of life, for the love of family and friends, and for your constant presence in our lives. Help us to cultivate a spirit of thanksgiving, O Lord, that we may always be mindful of your goodness. Amen.

Activity: Keeping a Gratitude Journal

Start a gratitude journal today, where you can daily write down three things you are thankful for. It could be something as simple as a beautiful sunrise or a kind gesture from a friend. By intentionally focusing on the blessings in your life, you will cultivate a spirit of gratitude that will enrich your journey towards Easter.

Day 4: Celebrating Resurrection

Reflection: Embracing the Miracle of New Life

As we enter into Easter week, we are reminded of the central message of our faith: the resurrection of Jesus Christ. Reflect on John 11:25-26, where Jesus declares, "I am the resurrection and the life. The one who believes in me will live, even though they die." Contemplate the miracle of new life that Easter represents, not just for Jesus, but for all who believe in Him. Consider how the resurrection offers hope and renewal in every aspect of our lives.

Prayer: Rejoicing in the Gift of Salvation

Gracious God, we rejoice in the gift of salvation made possible through the resurrection of your Son, Jesus Christ. Thank you for the promise of new life and the hope that it brings. Fill our hearts with joy and gratitude as we celebrate the miracle of Easter. Amen.

Activity: Decorating Easter Eggs

Engage in the tradition of decorating Easter eggs today as a symbol of new life and resurrection. Gather your family or friends and spend time creating beautiful designs on eggs using various colors and patterns. As you decorate, reflect on the significance of Easter and the hope it brings to the world. Display your decorated eggs as a reminder of the miracle of resurrection.

Day 5: Living in Light

Reflection: Walking in the Light of Christ

In a world filled with darkness, Jesus calls us to be the light. Reflect on Matthew 5:14-16, where Jesus says, "You are the light of the world...let your light shine before others, that they may see your good deeds and glorify your Father in heaven." Consider how you can shine the light of Christ in your daily life, bringing hope and encouragement to those around you.

Prayer: Seeking Guidance in Times of Darkness

Heavenly Father, in times of darkness, we turn to you as the source of light and guidance. Illuminate our path, O Lord, and lead us in the way of truth and righteousness. Help us to be beacons of your light, shining brightly in a world that desperately needs hope. Amen.

Activity: Lighting a Candle of Hope

Light a candle today as a symbolic gesture of hope and faith in the midst of darkness. As you watch the flame flicker and dance, reflect on the hope that Jesus brings into our lives. Offer prayers for those who are struggling and in need of light and hope.

Let the candle serve as a reminder of the light of Christ shining in the darkness.

Day 6: Extending Forgiveness

Reflection: Embracing the Power of Forgiveness

Forgiveness is a central theme of Easter, as Jesus' death and resurrection offer us the ultimate forgiveness for our sins. Reflect on Colossians 3:13, where it urges us to forgive as the Lord forgave us. Consider the power of forgiveness to heal and restore relationships, both with God and with others.

Prayer: Granting Forgiveness and Reconciliation

Merciful God, we thank you for the gift of forgiveness made possible through the sacrifice of your Son, Jesus Christ. Help us to extend that same forgiveness to others, releasing bitterness and resentment from our hearts. Grant us the grace to reconcile with those who have wronged us, just as you have reconciled us to yourself. Amen.

Activity: Writing a Letter of Forgiveness

Take time today to write a letter of forgiveness to someone who has hurt or wronged you in the past. Be honest about your feelings and express your desire to let go of any anger or resentment. You don't necessarily need to send the letter; the act of writing it can be cathartic and healing. Release the burden of unforgiveness and experience the freedom that comes from extending grace to others.

Day 7: Nurturing Seeds of Faith

Reflection: Cultivating Faith through Daily Practice

Faith is like a seed that needs to be nurtured and cultivated in order to grow. Reflect on Luke 8:11-15, the Parable of the Sower, where Jesus teaches about the importance of fertile soil for seeds to take root and flourish. Consider how daily practices such as prayer, scripture reading, and worship can create fertile ground for your faith to grow.

Prayer: Seeking Strength to Nurture Our Spiritual Growth

Heavenly Father, we come before you seeking strength and guidance to nurture our spiritual growth. Help us to cultivate a deep and abiding faith that is rooted in your love and grace. Grant us the wisdom to prioritize daily practices that will strengthen our relationship with you. Amen.

Activity: Planting a Garden of Faith

Take time today to physically plant a garden of faith. Whether it's in your backyard, a small plot of land, or even a few pots on your windowsill, plant flowers or herbs as a tangible representation of your faith. As you tend to your garden, reflect on how you can cultivate your spiritual life with the same care and attention.

Day 8: Watering Our Souls

Reflection: Quenching Our Spiritual Thirst

Just as plants need water to grow, our souls thirst for spiritual nourishment. Reflect on Psalm 42:1-2, where it describes the longing of the soul for God's presence like a deer panting for streams of water. Consider how you can quench your spiritual thirst through prayer, meditation, and communion with God.

Prayer: Drinking Deeply from the Well of Grace

Gracious God, you are the source of living water that satisfies our deepest thirst. Quench our spiritual thirst, O Lord, with your abundant grace and love. Fill us to overflowing with your Holy Spirit, that we may be refreshed and renewed in our faith journey. Amen.

Activity: Meditation and Mindfulness Exercise

Engage in a meditation and mindfulness exercise today to water your soul. Find a quiet place where you can sit comfortably and focus on your breath. Allow your thoughts to come and go without judgment, simply observing them with curiosity. As you practice mindfulness, open your heart to God's presence and guidance, allowing His peace to wash over you.

Day 9: Bearing Fruit

Reflection: Reflecting on the Fruits of the Spirit

As followers of Christ, we are called to bear fruit that reflects the character of God. Reflect on Galatians 5:22-23, where it describes the fruits of the Spirit: love, joy, peace, patience, kindness, goodness, faithfulness, gentleness, and self-control. Consider how these fruits are manifest in your life and where you can cultivate them further.

Prayer: Asking for Guidance in Bearing Good Fruit

Holy Spirit, guide us in bearing good fruit that honors and glorifies you. Teach us to love as you love, to bring joy and peace wherever we go, and to demonstrate patience and kindness in all circumstances. Fill us with your presence, that we may bear fruit that lasts. Amen.

Activity: Volunteering or Performing Acts of Kindness

Put your faith into action today by volunteering or performing acts of kindness for others. Whether it's serving at a local soup kitchen, visiting the elderly, or helping a neighbor in need, look for opportunities to spread love and compassion. As you engage in these acts of service, reflect on how you are bearing fruit that reflects the love of Christ to the world.

Day 10: Receiving the Spirit

Reflection: Opening Our Hearts to Receive the Spirit

Pentecost marks the outpouring of the Holy Spirit upon the disciples, empowering them for ministry and mission. Reflect on Acts 2:1-4, where the Spirit descends like tongues of fire, filling the believers with boldness and power. Consider how you can open your heart to receive the Holy Spirit afresh, inviting His guidance and presence into your life.

Prayer: Inviting the Holy Spirit to Guide Our Lives

Holy Spirit, we invite you to dwell within us, guiding us in all that we do. Fill us with your wisdom and understanding, that we may discern your will and follow your leading. Empower us to live as faithful witnesses of your love and grace. Amen.

Activity: Creating a Prayer Corner in Our Home

Designate a quiet corner in your home as a sacred space for prayer and reflection. Decorate it with candles, a small table or shelf for sacred objects, and comfortable seating. Spend time each day in this space, communing with God and listening for the promptings of the Holy Spirit. Let it be a tangible reminder of your commitment to invite the Spirit into your life.

Day 11: Empowered for Mission

Reflection: Answering the Call to Spread the Good News

As recipients of the Holy Spirit, we are called to be witnesses of the gospel and to share the good news with others. Reflect on Matthew 28:19-20, where Jesus commissions his disciples to go and make disciples of all nations. Consider how you can answer the call to spread the good news in your own sphere of influence.

Prayer: Empowering Us to Serve Others with Love

Gracious God, empower us to serve others with love and compassion, just as Jesus did during his earthly ministry. Fill us with your Spirit, that we may be bold and courageous in sharing the gospel message. Use us as instruments of your peace and agents of transformation in the world. Amen.

Activity: Finding Ways to Serve in Our Community

Look for opportunities to serve others in your community today. Whether it's volunteering at a local shelter, participating in a service project, or simply reaching out to a neighbor in need, seek ways to demonstrate God's love in tangible ways. As you serve others, reflect on how you are fulfilling your mission as a disciple of Christ.

Day 12: Continuing the Journey

Reflection: Reflecting on Our Spiritual Growth

As we conclude this devotional journey, take time to reflect on your spiritual growth and transformation. Consider the ways in which you have grown closer to God and how your faith has deepened over the past weeks. Reflect on Philippians 1:6, where it assures us that God will continue the good work He has started in us until it is completed on the day of Christ Jesus.

Prayer: Committing to Continued Growth and Transformation

Heavenly Father, we thank you for the journey of faith we have embarked upon in these past weeks. As we continue our spiritual journey, we commit ourselves to continued growth and transformation in Christ. May your Spirit continue to work in us, shaping us into vessels of your love and grace. Amen.

Activity: Setting Spiritual Goals for the Future

Take time today to prayerfully consider what spiritual goals you would like to set for yourself in the future. These could be related to prayer, scripture reading, serving others, or any other aspect of your spiritual life. Write them down and commit them to God, trusting that He will help you to achieve them in His timing.

Day 13: Seeking Wisdom

Reflection: Embracing the Wisdom of God

Wisdom is more than just knowledge; it's the discernment to apply knowledge rightly in our lives. As we seek wisdom, we align ourselves with the ways of God and gain insight into His plans and purposes. Proverbs 2:6 reminds us, "For the Lord gives wisdom; from his mouth come knowledge and understanding." Reflect on how embracing God's wisdom can lead to a more fulfilling and purposeful life.

Prayer: Seeking God's Guidance and Understanding

Heavenly Father, grant us wisdom as we navigate the complexities of life. Open our hearts and minds to receive your guidance and understanding. Help us to discern your will and to walk in your ways. May your wisdom illuminate our path and lead us closer to you each day. Amen.

Activity: Studying a Book of Wisdom (e.g., Proverbs)

Take time today to delve into a book of wisdom, such as Proverbs. Choose a passage that speaks to you and meditate on its message. Consider how you can apply the wisdom found in these scriptures to your own life. Whether it's seeking guidance on relationships, finances, or decision-making, the wisdom of God's word has timeless truths to offer.

Day 14: Trusting in God's Provision

Reflection: Trusting God's Faithfulness

In times of uncertainty or scarcity, it can be challenging to trust that God will provide. Yet, throughout scripture, we see His faithfulness demonstrated time and time again. Reflect on Matthew 6:26, where Jesus reminds us of God's care for the birds of the air, and how much more He cares for us. Trusting in God's faithfulness allows us to release our worries and anxieties and rest in His provision.

Prayer: Surrendering Our Worries and Needs to God

Dear God, we acknowledge that you are our provider, and we trust in your unfailing love and faithfulness. Help us to surrender our worries and needs to you, knowing that you will always provide for us according to your riches in glory. Strengthen our faith and increase our trust in your provision, even in the midst of uncertainty. Amen.

Activity: Practicing Generosity and Sharing with Others

As an expression of trust in God's provision, look for opportunities to practice generosity today. Whether it's donating to a charity, helping a neighbor in need, or simply offering a word of encouragement, seek ways to share with others what God has graciously given you. In giving, we not only bless others but also demonstrate our trust in God's abundant provision.

Day 15: Walking in Obedience

Reflection: Surrendering to God's Will

Obedience is a foundational aspect of our faith journey. It's about aligning our will with God's and willingly submitting to His authority. Reflect on 1 Samuel 15:22, where Samuel declares, "To obey is better than sacrifice." Consider areas of your life where obedience to God's commands may require sacrifice or stepping out of your comfort zone. Surrendering to God's will leads to blessings beyond measure.

Prayer: Asking for Strength to Obey God's Commands

Gracious Father, give us the strength and courage to obey your commands wholeheartedly. Help us to trust in your wisdom and goodness, even when obedience requires sacrifice or goes against our natural inclinations. May our lives be a testimony to your faithfulness and grace as we walk in obedience to your will. Amen.

Activity: Obeying God's Word in Daily Actions

Put your faith into action today by intentionally obeying God's word in your daily life. Whether it's forgiving someone who has wronged you, speaking words of kindness and encouragement, or resisting temptation, seek to align your actions with God's commands. Each act of obedience draws you closer to Him and strengthens your faith journey.

Day 16: Loving Our Neighbors

Reflection: Demonstrating Christ's Love to Others

Jesus taught us to love our neighbors as ourselves, showing compassion and kindness to all. Reflect on Luke 10:25-37, the parable of the Good Samaritan, and consider how you can demonstrate Christ's love to those around you. Look for opportunities to reach out and make a difference in someone's life today.

Prayer: Blessing Those Around Us with Love

Heavenly Father, help us to see others through your eyes and to love them with your heart. Teach us to be instruments of your love and compassion, blessing those around us with acts of kindness and grace. May our words and actions reflect the love of Christ and draw others closer to you. Amen.

Activity: Reaching Out to Someone in Need

Take intentional steps today to reach out to someone in need. It could be a friend going through a difficult time, a neighbor who could use a helping hand, or a stranger in need of encouragement. Whether through a kind word, a thoughtful gesture, or practical assistance, let your love and compassion shine brightly.

Day 17: Showing Kindness

Reflection: Practicing Acts of Kindness

Kindness is a powerful expression of love that can brighten someone's day and bring hope to their heart. Reflect on Ephesians 4:32, which encourages us to be kind and compassionate to one another, forgiving each other, just as in Christ God forgave you. Consider how you can intentionally practice acts of kindness in your interactions with others.

Prayer: Asking for Opportunities to Show Kindness

Lord, open our eyes to the needs of those around us and give us opportunities to show kindness and compassion. Help us to be mindful of the struggles and challenges others may be facing and to offer words and deeds of kindness that uplift and encourage. Guide us by your Spirit to be channels of your love in the world. Amen.

Activity: Random Acts of Kindness Challenge

Challenge yourself to perform random acts of kindness throughout the day. It could be as simple as holding the door open for someone, paying for the coffee of the person behind you in line, or leaving an encouraging note for a colleague. Let each act of kindness be a reflection of God's love and grace in action.

Day 18: Extending Mercy

Reflection: Embracing the Gift of God's Mercy

Mercy is a precious gift that God freely offers to us, despite our shortcomings and failures. Reflect on Lamentations 3:22-23, which reminds us of the Lord's great love and compassion that never fails. Consider how you can extend the same mercy and forgiveness to those who have wronged you, following Christ's example of grace.

Prayer: Seeking Forgiveness and Offering Mercy

Gracious Father, thank you for your abundant mercy and forgiveness towards us. Help us to forgive others as you have forgiven us, releasing bitterness and resentment from our hearts. Grant us the strength to extend mercy to those who have wronged us, showing them the same grace that you have shown us. Amen.

Activity: Forgiving Someone Who Has Wronged Us

Take a courageous step today to extend forgiveness to someone who has wronged you. It may not be easy, but remember that forgiveness is a gift that sets both the forgiver and the forgiven free. Choose to release any grudges or resentments, and instead, offer mercy and reconciliation. In doing so, you reflect the transformative power of God's love and grace.

Day 19: Building Unity

Reflection: Fostering Unity Among Believers

Unity among believers is crucial for the advancement of God's kingdom. Reflect on Psalm 133:1, which says, "How good and pleasant it is when God's people live together in unity!" Consider the importance of fostering unity in your church community and how you can contribute to creating an atmosphere of love, harmony, and mutual respect.

Prayer: Praying for Unity in the Body of Christ

Heavenly Father, we pray for unity among believers, both within our local church and throughout the body of Christ worldwide. Help us to set aside our differences and work together in love and humility, for the sake of your kingdom. May our unity be a testimony to the world of your power and grace. Amen.

Activity: Participating in a Church Fellowship Event

Take part in a church fellowship event or activity that promotes unity and camaraderie among believers. Whether it's a potluck dinner, a small group gathering, or a service project, use this opportunity to build relationships, strengthen bonds, and experience the joy of community in Christ.

Day 20: Honoring Family

Reflection: Valuing and Honoring Family Relationships

Family is a precious gift from God, and honoring our family members is a reflection of our love for

Him. Reflect on Ephesians 6:2-3, which instructs us to honor our parents, and consider the significance of valuing and cherishing our family relationships. Think about ways you can demonstrate love and respect towards your family members.

Prayer: Blessing Our Family Members with God's Love

Lord, we thank you for the gift of family and the love that binds us together. Help us to honor and cherish our family members, showing them the same love and grace that you have shown us. Bless each member of our family with your presence, protection, and peace. Amen.

Activity: Spending Quality Time with Family

Make intentional efforts to spend quality time with your family today. Whether it's sharing a meal together, going for a walk, or engaging in meaningful conversations, prioritize building strong connections and fostering unity within your family. Let your actions demonstrate love, care, and appreciation for each member of your family.

Day 21: Reconciliation and Restoration

Reflection: Pursuing Reconciliation in Broken Relationships

Reconciliation is at the heart of the gospel message, and God calls us to be agents of reconciliation in our relationships. Reflect on 2 Corinthians 5:18-19, which speaks of God reconciling us to Himself through Christ and entrusting us with the ministry of reconciliation. Consider any broken relationships in your life and how you can pursue reconciliation and restoration.

Prayer: Seeking Healing and Restoration in Relationships

Lord, we lift up to you any broken relationships in our lives and ask for your healing and restoration. Give us the humility to seek reconciliation, the courage to extend forgiveness, and the grace to rebuild trust. May your love and grace abound in our relationships, bringing healing and wholeness where there is brokenness. Amen.

Activity: Reaching Out to Reconcile with Someone Estranged

Take proactive steps today to reach out to someone with whom you have a strained or estranged relationship. Extend an olive branch of peace, express your desire for reconciliation, and offer forgiveness where needed. Even if reconciliation does not happen immediately, take comfort in knowing that you have obeyed God's call to pursue peace and unity.

Day 22: Sharing the Gospel

Reflection: Boldly Sharing the Good News of Jesus Christ

The gospel is the message of salvation and hope for all humanity. Reflect on Mark 16:15, where Jesus commands His disciples to "Go into all the world and preach the gospel to all creation." Consider how you can boldly proclaim the good news of Jesus Christ to those around you, both through your words and actions.

Prayer: Asking for Courage and Boldness in Witnessing

Lord, grant us the courage and boldness to share the gospel with others, even in the face of opposition or fear. Fill us with your Holy Spirit and give us the words to speak as we testify to your saving grace and love. Use us as instruments of your gospel message, that many may come to know and believe in you. Amen.

Activity: Sharing Your Testimony with Someone

Take the opportunity today to share your personal testimony of faith with someone. Whether it's a friend, family member, coworker, or stranger, share how God has transformed your life through His love and grace. Your testimony has the power to touch hearts and lead others into a deeper relationship with Christ.

Day 23: Planting Seeds of Hope

Reflection: Bringing Hope to Those in Despair

In a world filled with darkness and despair, we are called to be bearers of hope. Reflect on Romans 15:13, which says, "May the God of hope fill you with all joy and peace as you trust in him, so that you may overflow with hope by the power of the Holy Spirit." Consider how you can bring hope to those who are struggling and in need of encouragement.

Prayer: Interceding for Those in Need of Hope

Heavenly Father, we lift up to you those who are struggling and in despair, and we ask for your comfort and hope to fill their hearts. Use us as vessels of your love and encouragement, that we may bring light into the darkness and hope to the hopeless. May your presence be felt by all who are in need. Amen.

Activity: Encouraging Someone Who Is Going Through Difficult Times

Reach out to someone who is going through a challenging season and offer words of encouragement and support. Whether it's a listening ear, a heartfelt note, or a simple act of kindness, let your actions convey hope and reassurance. Your words and gestures can be a source of strength and comfort to those in need.

Day 24: Cultivating Joy

Reflection: Choosing Joy in All Circumstances

Joy is a fruit of the Spirit that transcends circumstances and is rooted in our relationship with God. Reflect on Philippians 4:4, which says, "Rejoice in the Lord always. I will say it again: Rejoice!" Consider how you can cultivate a spirit of joy in your life, regardless of the challenges or difficulties you may face.

Prayer: Rejoicing in the Lord Always

Lord, we thank you for the gift of joy that comes from knowing you and walking in your ways. Help us to rejoice in you always, even in the midst of trials and tribulations. Fill us with your joy and peace that surpasses all understanding, and let it overflow into the lives of those around us. Amen.

Activity: Spreading Joy Through Acts of Celebration

Celebrate the goodness of God and the blessings in your life by engaging in acts of celebration. Whether it's hosting a praise and worship night, throwing a party to celebrate answered prayers, or simply rejoicing in the small victories of each day, let your joy be contagious and spread to those around you.

Day 25: Counting Blessings

Reflection: Recognizing God's Goodness

Take a moment to reflect on the countless blessings God has bestowed upon you. Consider Psalm 103:2, which says, "Bless the Lord, O my soul, and forget not all his benefits." Think about the ways God has shown His goodness and faithfulness in your life, and express gratitude for His provision and care.

Prayer: Offering Thanks for God's Blessings

Heavenly Father, we thank you for your abundant blessings and provision in our lives. Help us to cultivate a heart of gratitude and to recognize your goodness in all things. May our lives be a testimony to your faithfulness, as we give thanks for your countless blessings each day. Amen.

Activity: Keeping a Gratitude Journal

Start a gratitude journal today, where you can record the blessings and goodness you experience each day. Take time to write down at least three things you are thankful for, whether big or small. Cultivating a habit of gratitude through journaling can transform your perspective and increase your joy.

Day 26: Expressing Thankfulness

Reflection: Gratitude in Action

Gratitude is not just a feeling but an action that flows from a thankful heart. Reflect on 1 Thessalonians 5:18, which says, "Give thanks in all circumstances; for this is the will of God in Christ Jesus for you." Consider how you can express your gratitude to God and others through words and deeds.

Prayer: Thanking God for His Faithfulness

Lord, we thank you for your faithfulness and goodness towards us. Help us to express our gratitude to you and to those around us, acknowledging the blessings and provisions we receive each day. May our words and actions reflect the thankfulness of our hearts, bringing glory to your name. Amen.

Activity: Writing Thank You Notes

Take time today to write thank you notes to people who have blessed or helped you in some way. Whether it's a friend who offered a listening ear, a coworker who went above and beyond, or a family member who showed love and support, let them know how much you appreciate them. Your words of thanks can brighten someone's day and deepen your relationships.

Day 27: Gratitude in Adversity

Reflection: Finding Gratitude in Hardship

Even in the midst of trials and adversity, we can find reasons to be grateful. Reflect on James 1:2-3, which says, "Consider it pure joy, my brothers and sisters, whenever you face trials of many kinds, because you know that the testing of your faith produces perseverance." Consider how challenges can lead to growth and deepen your gratitude for God's faithfulness.

Prayer: Trusting God's Sovereignty

Heavenly Father, we thank you for your sovereignty and faithfulness, even in the midst of difficult circumstances. Help us to trust in your goodness and to find reasons to be grateful, even when life is hard. Give us the strength to persevere and the faith to see your hand at work in all things. Amen.

Activity: Finding Silver Linings

Challenge yourself to find silver linings in the midst of adversity today. Look for small blessings or moments of grace that bring light into the darkness. Whether it's a lesson learned, a relationship strengthened, or a newfound sense of resilience, let these silver linings inspire gratitude in your heart.

Day 28: Seeking Rest

Reflection: Finding Rest in God

In the midst of life's busyness and chaos, God invites us to find rest in His presence. Reflect on Matthew 11:28, where Jesus says, "Come to me, all you who are weary and burdened, and I will give you rest." Consider the importance of prioritizing rest and seeking refuge in God's loving arms.

Prayer: Resting in God's Peace

Lord, we thank you for the rest and peace you offer to those who come to you. Help us to cast our cares upon you and find refuge in your presence. Grant us the rest we need for our bodies, minds, and spirits, that we may be renewed and refreshed to continue our journey with you. Amen.

Activity: Practicing Sabbath Rest

Set aside time today to practice Sabbath rest, where you intentionally rest from work and busyness and devote yourself to God and His presence. Whether it's through prayer, meditation, worship, or simply enjoying God's creation, let this time of rest rejuvenate your soul and strengthen your connection with Him.

Day 29: Trusting in God's Provision

Reflection: Relying on God's Faithfulness

God is faithful to provide for our every need, even in the midst of uncertainty and scarcity. Reflect on Philippians 4:19, which says, "And my God will supply every need of yours according to his riches in glory in Christ Jesus." Consider how you can trust in God's provision and rely on His faithfulness in all circumstances.

Prayer: Trusting God's Provision

Heavenly Father, we thank you for your abundant provision and faithfulness in our lives. Help us to trust in your promises and to rely on your provision, knowing that you will always provide for our needs according to your riches in glory. Increase our faith and dependence on you, that we may experience the fullness of your blessings. Amen.

Activity: Reflecting on God's Provision

Take time today to reflect on the ways God has provided for you in the past. Consider keeping a journal of His faithfulness, writing down instances where He has met your needs and answered your prayers. As you meditate on His provision, let it strengthen your trust in Him for the future.

Day 30: Finding Strength in Weakness

Reflection: Experiencing God's Strength

In our moments of weakness, God offers His strength to sustain us and carry us through. Reflect on 2 Corinthians 12:9-10, where Paul writes, "For when I am weak, then I am strong." Consider how God's strength is made perfect in our weakness, and how we can find hope and courage in Him.

Prayer: Surrendering to God's Strength

Lord, we thank you for your strength that sustains us in our moments of weakness. Help us to surrender our weaknesses to you and to rely on your strength to carry us through. May your power be made perfect in our weakness, that we may glorify you in all we do. Amen.

Activity: Drawing Strength from Scripture

Find strength and encouragement today by immersing yourself in God's word. Choose scriptures that speak to your current circumstances or struggles, and meditate on them deeply. Allow God's promises and truths to fill you with hope, courage, and strength to face whatever challenges lie ahead.

Day 31: Renewing Our Minds

Reflection: Transforming Our Minds by the Renewal of God's Word

Our minds are continually bombarded with worldly influences and distractions, but God calls us to renew our minds with His truth. Reflect on Romans 12:2, which urges us not to conform to the patterns of this world but to be transformed by the renewing of our minds. Consider how immersing ourselves in God's Word can transform our thoughts and perspectives.

Prayer: Asking God to Renew Our Thoughts and Perspectives

Heavenly Father, we thank you for the power of your Word to transform our minds and hearts. Renew our thoughts and perspectives, Lord, that we may align them with your truth and purposes. Help us to discern what is pleasing to you and to walk in obedience to your will. Amen.

Activity: Engaging in Reflective Journaling on Spiritual Growth

Take time today to engage in reflective journaling on your spiritual growth journey. Reflect on how God has been at work in your life, the areas where you've experienced growth, and the areas where you may need renewal. Write down insights, prayers, and action steps as you seek to align your mind with God's truth.

Day 32: Reflecting on God's Love

Reflection: Meditating on the Depth of God's Love for Us

God's love for us is unfathomable, beyond comprehension, and without conditions. Reflect on Ephesians 3:17-19, which speaks of the breadth, length, height, and depth of God's love that surpasses knowledge. Meditate on the depth of God's love for you personally, and allow it to sink deep into your heart.

Prayer: Expressing Gratitude for God's Unconditional Love

Gracious God, we thank you for your overwhelming love that knows no bounds. Thank you for loving us unconditionally, despite our flaws and failures. Help us to grasp the depth of your love more fully and to live in the reality of your love each day. Amen.

Activity: Writing a Love Letter to God, Pouring Out Your Heart

Express your love and gratitude to God by writing Him a heartfelt love letter. Pour out your thoughts, feelings, and expressions of love to Him, acknowledging His faithfulness, goodness, and grace in your life. Allow this exercise to deepen your connection with God and cultivate a greater awareness of His presence and love.

Day 33: Revisiting Our Purpose

Reflection: Realigning Our Lives with God's Purpose for Us

God has a unique purpose and plan for each of our lives, and it's essential to regularly revisit and realign ourselves with His purposes. Reflect on

Jeremiah 29:11, which assures us that God has plans to prosper us and not to harm us, plans to give us hope and a future. Consider how your life aligns with God's purposes and where adjustments may be needed.

Prayer: Seeking Clarity and Direction for Our Life's Purpose

Lord, we seek clarity and direction for our lives, knowing that you have a purpose and plan for each of us. Help us to discern your will and to walk in obedience to your calling. Guide us in aligning our lives with your purposes and empower us to fulfill the destiny you have for us. Amen.

Activity: Reflecting on Past Accomplishments and Future Goals

Take time today to reflect on past accomplishments and milestones in your life, as well as to set goals and aspirations for the future. Consider how your past experiences have shaped you and how God may be leading you forward. Write down specific goals and action steps as you seek to live out God's purpose for your life.

Day 34: Committing to Holiness

Reflection: Pursuing Holiness in Every Area of Our Lives

Holiness is the call of every believer, to be set apart for God's purposes and to reflect His character in all we do. Reflect on 1 Peter 1:15-16, which urges us to be holy as God is holy. Consider how you can pursue holiness in every area of your life, surrendering your desires and aligning yourself with God's will.

Prayer: Surrendering Ourselves to God's Sanctifying Work

Lord, we surrender ourselves to your sanctifying work in our lives, knowing that you desire for us to be holy as you are holy. Help us to walk in obedience to your commands and to live lives that honor and glorify you. Sanctify us by your truth, that we may be vessels of honor fit for your use. Amen.

Activity: Making a Personal Commitment to Live a Holy Life

Take time today to make a personal commitment to live a holy life before God. Write down specific areas where you need to surrender to His will and commit to making changes in your thoughts, words, and actions. Share your commitment with a trusted friend or mentor for accountability and support.

Day 35: Embracing Spiritual Disciplines

Reflection: Incorporating Spiritual Disciplines into Our Daily Routine

Spiritual disciplines are essential practices that help us grow closer to God and deepen our relationship with Him. Reflect on Psalm 119:105, which says, "Your word is a lamp to my feet and a light to my path." Consider how you can incorporate disciplines such as prayer, Bible study, fasting, and meditation into your daily routine.

Prayer: Asking for Discipline and Diligence in Spiritual Practices

Heavenly Father, we ask for the discipline and diligence to engage in spiritual practices that draw us closer to you. Help us to prioritize time with you each day, seeking your presence through prayer, meditation on your word, and other spiritual disciplines. May our hearts be attuned to your leading and our lives be transformed by your Spirit. Amen.

Activity: Creating a Personal Spiritual Disciplines Plan

Create a personal spiritual disciplines plan outlining the spiritual practices you want to incorporate into your daily life. Set specific goals and action steps for each discipline, along with a schedule for implementation. Review your plan regularly and adjust as needed to ensure consistency and growth in your spiritual journey.

Day 36: Surrendering All to God

Reflection: Letting Go and Surrendering Control to God

Surrender is a key aspect of the Christian life, as we relinquish control and trust in God's sovereignty. Reflect on Proverbs 3:5-6, which instructs us to trust in the Lord with all our hearts and lean not on our own understanding. Consider areas of your life where you may be holding onto control and surrender them to God's will.

Prayer: Yielding Our Lives Completely to God's Will

Lord, we yield our lives completely to your will, trusting in your perfect plan and purpose for us. Help us to let go of our own desires and ambitions, and to surrender to your leading and direction in all things. May our lives be a living sacrifice, holy and pleasing to you. Amen.

Activity: Symbolically Surrendering Personal Items as a Sign of Surrender

As a symbolic act of surrender, choose a personal item or possession that represents an area of your life you are struggling to relinquish control over. Offer it up to God as a sign of your willingness to surrender all to Him. Whether it's a cherished possession, a habit, or a dream, let go and trust in God's providence and care.

Day 37: Empowering Others

Reflection: Equipping and Empowering Others for Kingdom Work

As followers of Christ, we are called to equip and empower others for the work of the kingdom. Reflect on Ephesians 4:12, which speaks of equipping the saints for the work of ministry. Consider how you can come alongside others, empowering them to fulfill their God-given purposes and gifts.

Prayer: Asking for Opportunities to Empower and Encourage Others

Heavenly Father, we pray for opportunities to empower and encourage others in their faith journey. Open our eyes to see the needs of those around us, and give us the wisdom and discernment to offer support and guidance. May we be vessels of your love and grace, empowering others to walk in the fullness of their calling. Amen.

Activity: Mentoring or Discipling Someone in Their Faith Journey

Take intentional steps today to mentor or disciple someone in their faith journey. This could involve meeting for coffee, having a Bible study together, or simply offering a listening ear and words of encouragement. Invest in building up others spiritually and helping them grow closer to God.

Day 38: Encouraging the Faint-hearted

Reflection: Strengthening and Uplifting Those Who Are Discouraged

In times of discouragement, we are called to come alongside our brothers and sisters in Christ, offering support and encouragement. Reflect on 1 Thessalonians 5:11, which urges us to encourage one another and build each other up. Consider how you can be a source of strength and comfort to those who are faint-hearted.

Prayer: Interceding for Those in Need of Encouragement

Lord, we lift up those who are discouraged and faint-hearted, asking for your comfort and strength to surround them. Use us as instruments of your peace and encouragement, that we may uplift and support those who are struggling. Help us to be sensitive to the needs of others and to offer words of hope and encouragement. Amen.

Activity: Sending Encouraging Notes or Messages to Those in Need

Take time today to send encouraging notes or messages to those who are in need of upliftment. Whether it's a friend going through a tough time, a family member facing challenges, or a colleague feeling overwhelmed, reach out with words of love, hope, and encouragement. Your kindness and support can make a significant difference in someone's day.

Day 39: Sharing Our Testimony

Reflection: Sharing the Story of God's Work in Our Lives

Our testimonies are powerful tools for sharing the gospel and encouraging others in their faith. Reflect on Revelation 12:11, which speaks of overcoming by the blood of the Lamb and the word of our testimony. Consider the ways God has worked in your life and how sharing your testimony can impact others for Christ.

Prayer: Asking for Boldness and Clarity in Sharing Our Testimony

Heavenly Father, grant us boldness and clarity as we share our testimonies with others. Help us to articulate your work in our lives in a way that glorifies you and points others to Jesus. Give us opportunities and open doors for sharing, and may our testimonies be a source of inspiration and encouragement to those who hear them. Amen.

Activity: Sharing Our Testimony with a Friend, Family Member, or Group

Take a step of faith today by sharing your testimony with a friend, family member, or group of believers. You can do this in person, over the phone, or even through writing or social media. Share about God's faithfulness, provision, and redemption in your life, and invite others to experience His grace and love firsthand.

Day 40: Cultivating a Heart of Gratitude

Reflection: Practicing Gratitude in Every Circumstance

Gratitude is a powerful practice that shifts our focus from what we lack to the abundance of blessings around us. Reflect on 1 Thessalonians 5:18, which encourages us to give thanks in all circumstances. Consider how you can cultivate a heart of gratitude, even in the midst of challenges and trials.

Prayer: Thanking God for His Goodness and Provision

Heavenly Father, we thank you for your goodness and provision in our lives. Help us to develop a habit of gratitude, acknowledging your blessings and faithfulness each day. Teach us to see the beauty in every circumstance and to respond with thanksgiving, knowing that you are always working for our good. Amen.

Activity: Keeping a Gratitude Journal and Recording Blessings Daily

Start a gratitude journal today and commit to recording at least three blessings each day. Take time to reflect on the things you're thankful for, both big and small, and write them down as a reminder of God's faithfulness and provision in your life. Review your journal regularly to cultivate a heart of gratitude.

Day 41: Overflowing with Generosity

Reflection: Giving Generously from a Heart of Abundance

Generosity flows from a heart that recognizes God's abundant blessings and seeks to share them with others. Reflect on 2 Corinthians 9:6-7, which encourages cheerful and generous giving. Consider how you can cultivate a spirit of generosity in your life, both with your resources and your time.

Prayer: Asking God to Multiply Our Resources for His Kingdom Purposes

Lord, we pray that you would multiply our resources for your kingdom purposes. Help us to be faithful stewards of what you've entrusted to us, and to use our time, talents, and resources to bless others and advance your kingdom. May our generosity be a reflection of your love and grace. Amen.

Activity: Finding Opportunities to Give Generously to Others in Need

Look for opportunities today to give generously to those in need, whether it's through financial support, acts of service, or words of encouragement. Seek out organizations or individuals who are doing God's work in the world and consider how you can partner with them in their mission. Step out in faith and trust God to use your generosity to make a difference in the lives of others.

Day 42: Investing in Eternal Rewards

Reflection: Prioritizing Kingdom Investments Over Earthly Treasures

Our earthly possessions are temporary, but the investments we make in God's kingdom have eternal significance. Reflect on Matthew 6:19-21, which speaks of storing up treasures in heaven. Consider how you can realign your priorities to focus more on investing in eternal rewards rather than accumulating earthly wealth.

Prayer: Seeking Wisdom in Stewarding Our Time, Talents, and Resources

Heavenly Father, grant us wisdom in stewarding our time, talents, and resources for your glory. Help us to recognize the eternal value of our investments in your kingdom and to prioritize them above earthly pursuits. Guide us in making decisions that honor you and further your kingdom purposes. Amen.

Activity: Evaluating Our Priorities and Making Adjustments for Kingdom Impact

Take time today to evaluate your priorities and consider whether they align with God's kingdom values. Identify areas where you may need to make adjustments to invest more in eternal rewards, such as spending more time in prayer and studying God's word, serving others, or supporting mission work. Make a plan to realign your priorities and take steps toward greater kingdom impact.

Day 43: Anticipating Christ's Return

Reflection: Eagerly Waiting for the Coming of Our Lord Jesus Christ

The return of Christ is a central theme in Christian faith and theology. Reflect on 1 Th

essalonians 4:16-17, which describes the Lord descending from heaven with a shout, and the dead in Christ rising first. Consider the hope and anticipation that fills the hearts of believers as they eagerly await the fulfillment of this promise.

Prayer: Longing for the Day When We Will Be United with Christ Forever

Heavenly Father, we long for the day when we will be united with Christ forever. As we eagerly await His return, fill our hearts with hope and anticipation. Help us to live each day in light of this blessed hope, eagerly anticipating the glorious moment when we will be with Him for eternity. Amen.

Activity: Studying End-Time Prophecies and Reflecting on Their Significance

Take time today to study end-time prophecies found in scripture, such as those in the book of Revelation and the teachings of Jesus in Matthew 24. Reflect on the significance of these prophecies and how they shape our understanding of Christ's return. Consider joining a study group or online forum to discuss these prophecies with other believers.

Day 44: Preparing Our Hearts

Reflection: Purifying Our Hearts and Lives in Anticipation of Christ's Return

In anticipation of Christ's return, we are called to purify our hearts and lives from sin. Reflect on 1 John 3:2-3, which speaks of the hope of seeing Christ and purifying ourselves just as He is pure. Consider areas of your life where you need to repent and seek God's cleansing and renewal.

Prayer: Repenting of Sin and Seeking God's Cleansing and Renewal

Lord, we confess our sins and shortcomings before you, knowing that you are faithful and just to forgive us and cleanse us from all unrighteousness. As we prepare for Christ's return, purify our hearts and lives, and make us holy as you are holy. Help us to live lives of repentance and renewal, constantly seeking to align ourselves with your will. Amen.

Activity: Participating in a Personal Spiritual Retreat for Reflection and Renewal

Set aside time today for a personal spiritual retreat, where you can engage in reflection, prayer, and renewal. Find a quiet place where you can spend uninterrupted time in God's presence, seeking His guidance and direction for your life. Use this time to confess sin, seek forgiveness, and renew your commitment to following Christ wholeheartedly.

Day 45: Watching and Praying

Reflection: Remaining Vigilant and Prayerful in Times of Waiting

As we await Christ's return, we are called to remain vigilant and prayerful, watching for signs of His coming. Reflect on Mark 13:32-37, where Jesus instructs His disciples to stay awake and be on guard, for no one knows the day or hour of His return. Consider how you can cultivate a watchful and prayerful attitude in your daily life.

Prayer: Keeping Alert and Praying Without Ceasing for God's Kingdom Purposes

Lord, help us to stay alert and vigilant, watching for signs of your coming kingdom. Teach us to pray without ceasing, interceding for your will to be done on earth as it is in heaven. May our hearts be attuned to your Spirit, and may we be faithful servants, ready and waiting for your return. Amen.

Activity: Establishing a Watchful Prayer Routine and Interceding for Current Events

Develop a watchful prayer routine where you set aside dedicated time each day to pray for God's kingdom purposes and the fulfillment of His promises. Intercede for current events, global issues, and the needs of others, asking God to work His will in every situation. Keep a prayer journal to record your petitions and God's answers, and be faithful in lifting up the concerns of the world to the throne of grace.

Day 46: Celebrating God's Faithfulness

Reflection: Reflecting on God's Faithfulness Throughout Salvation History

God's faithfulness is evident throughout salvation history, from the creation of the world to the redemption of humanity through Christ. Reflect on passages such as Psalm 100:5, which declares that the Lord is good, and His faithfulness endures forever. Consider the ways God has been faithful to you personally and to His people throughout history.

Prayer: Offering Praise and Worship for God's Unchanging Character

Gracious God, we thank you for your unwavering faithfulness throughout history. You are the same yesterday, today, and forever, and your faithfulness knows no bounds. We offer you praise and worship for your unchanging character and your steadfast love toward us. May our lives be a reflection of your faithfulness to the world. Amen.

Activity: Hosting a Celebration of God's Faithfulness with Family and Friends

Gather with family and friends to host a celebration of God's faithfulness. Share testimonies of His goodness and grace in your lives, sing worship songs of praise and thanksgiving, and enjoy fellowship together. Consider incorporating elements such as sharing a meal, praying together, and engaging in activities that remind you of God's faithfulness.

Day 47: Commemorating God's Miracles

Reflection: Remembering and Testifying to God's Miraculous Works

God has performed countless miracles throughout history, demonstrating His power and sovereignty. Reflect on passages such as Exodus 15:11, which declares that there is no one like God, who performs miracles and displays His power among the nations. Consider the miracles you have personally witnessed or heard about and how they have impacted your faith.

Prayer: Thanking God for His Miracles and Supernatural Interventions

Heavenly Father, we thank you for the miracles and supernatural interventions you have performed in our lives and in the world around us. You are the God of wonders, and your power knows no limits. We praise you for your mighty works and give you thanks for your continued presence and provision in our lives. Amen.

Activity: Creating a Memory Book or Collage of God's Miraculous Provisions

Create a memory book or collage featuring stories, pictures, and testimonies of God's miraculous provisions and interventions. Include personal accounts of answered prayers, healings, deliverances, and other supernatural experiences. Display this visual reminder of God's faithfulness in a prominent place where you can revisit it often and share it with others.

Day 48: Rejoicing in Eternal Victory

Reflection: Celebrating the Ultimate Victory of Christ Over Sin and Death

The ultimate victory we have in Christ is the triumph over sin and death through His death and resurrection. Reflect on passages such as 1 Corinthians 15:57, which declares that thanks be to God, who gives us the victory through our Lord Jesus Christ. Consider the implications of this victory for your life and eternity.

Prayer: Rejoicing in the Hope of Eternal Life and Resurrection

Lord Jesus, we rejoice in the hope of eternal life and resurrection that we have through your victory over sin and death. You have conquered the grave and secured our salvation, and for that, we are eternally grateful. May we live in the reality of this victory each day, knowing that nothing can separate us from your love. Amen.

Activity: Participating in a Worship Service Focused on the Victory of Christ

Attend a worship service or gathering focused on celebrating the victory of Christ over sin and death. Engage wholeheartedly in worship through singing, prayer, Scripture reading, and reflection on the significance of Christ's resurrection. Take time to thank God for His victory and recommit yourself to living in the light of this truth.

Day 49: Reflecting on the Journey

Reflection: Looking Back on the 50-Day Devotional Journey and Personal Growth

Take a moment to reflect on the 50-day devotional journey you've been on. Consider the lessons you've learned, the insights you've gained, and the ways in which your relationship with God has deepened. Reflect on passages such as Psalm 119:105, which speaks of God's word as a lamp to our feet and a light to our path, guiding us on our journey of faith.

Prayer: Thanking God for His Faithfulness Throughout the Journey

Heavenly Father, we thank you for your faithfulness throughout this 50-day devotional journey. You have been our constant companion, guiding us, strengthening us, and revealing your truth to us through your word. We praise you for your steadfast love and faithfulness, and we commit ourselves to continue following you with all our hearts. Amen.

Activity: Journaling Reflections on Lessons Learned and Spiritual Growth

Take time to journal your reflections on the lessons learned and the spiritual growth experienced during this journey. Write about moments of clarity, times of challenge, and experiences of God's presence.

Consider how you can apply these insights to your daily life moving forward and what steps you can take to continue growing in your faith.

Day 50: Committing to Ongoing Growth

Reflection: Making a Commitment to Continue Growing and Serving God

As we reach the final day of this devotional journey, commit yourself to ongoing growth and service in your walk with God. Reflect on Philippians 1:6, which assures us that He who began a good work in us will carry it on to completion until the day of Christ Jesus. Consider how you can continue to grow spiritually and serve God faithfully in the days ahead.

Prayer: Dedication to a Lifelong Journey of Faith, Service, and Transformation

Lord, as we come to the end of this devotional journey, we dedicate ourselves anew to a lifelong journey of faith, service, and transformation. May your Holy Spirit continue to work in us, shaping us into the image of Christ and empowering us to live lives that honor and glorify you. Help us to remain steadfast and faithful, always abounding in the work of the Lord. Amen.

Activity: Setting Goals for Continued Spiritual Growth and Kingdom Impact

Take time to prayerfully set goals for your continued spiritual growth and kingdom impact. Consider areas such as prayer, study of God's word, involvement in your church or community, and serving others. Write down specific, achievable goals and create a plan of action to help you stay accountable and focused on pursuing these goals.

CONCLUSION

As we come to the end of "3 Minutes a Day from Easter to Pentecost: A Daily Devotional with Reflections, Prayer, and Activities," we reflect on the journey we've embarked upon together. Over the past four weeks, we've delved into the significance of Easter, explored the themes of renewal, hope, and forgiveness, and celebrated the outpouring of the Holy Spirit at Pentecost.

Throughout this devotional, we've been reminded of the central message of our faith: the love and grace of God revealed to us through Jesus Christ. We've encountered scripture passages that have challenged and inspired us, prayers that have lifted our hearts to God, and activities that have encouraged us to put our faith into action.

But our journey doesn't end here. As we close this book, we are reminded that our walk with God is a lifelong journey of growth and transformation. The lessons we've learned and the experiences we've had in these pages are just the beginning of what God has in store for us.

As we move forward from Easter to Pentecost and beyond, may we continue to seek God's presence in our lives, to cultivate a deeper relationship with Him, and to bear witness to His love and grace in the world. May we be empowered by the Holy Spirit to live lives of faith, hope, and love, bringing light and healing wherever we go.

Thank you for joining us on this journey. May the words of this devotional continue to inspire and encourage you in your walk with God, and may you experience His presence and blessings in abundance each day.

May the grace of our Lord Jesus Christ, the love of God, and the fellowship of the Holy Spirit be with you always. Amen.

Made in United States
Orlando, FL
30 March 2024